Collateral Damage

DR. VERA GOODMAN

ISBN 978-1-0980-6939-1 (paperback)
ISBN 978-1-0980-6940-7 (hardcover)
ISBN 978-1-0980-6941-4 (digital)

Christian Faith Publishing, Inc.
832 Park Avenue
Meadville, PA 16335
www.christianfaithpublishing.com

Printed in the United States of America

My Prayer

Lord, thank You for another opportunity to be able to share my testimony. I've learned a long time ago how to remain grateful through the good and the bad times in life. I've learned that even when my heart is broken, I can still put all my trust in You. You always take me in Your arms in the midst of all of my suffering and assure me that everything is going to be all right. Sometimes I don't understand, but I trust You and I always will.

Thank You, God, for coming through for me even when some would call them little ways; but to me, in my times of feeling low in my spirit, the little gestures of love were huge! For that, Lord, I want to say thank You. Nothing that I do for You has ever been about fame or fortune, but only for You to get the glory through me.

Trials are coming from left and right, but the Word that You sent through the Priest of this house, "I Am, Still Is," lets me know that You are still *here* and You still *hear* me. So, God, because of Your love for me, I've decided to have peace and joy. I've decided to rise above my trials and take up my little crosses and follow You.

Your Daughter,
Vera

Contents

Introduction

While sitting in my living room thinking and just reminiscing, I began to thank God for preparing His people for such a time as this. For generations, our grandparents, our parents, and more importantly, the Word of God, warned us about these times. We refer to what I'm talking about as the last and evil days. We were fortunate enough at our local church to have a Revelation series taught by our pastor (and my husband), Bishop Dr. Jan D. Goodman Sr.

God had him break down the entire book of Revelation so that we could fully understand what we were about to face. It was taught line by line and precept by precept. It took a year and a half to complete the entire book of Revelation because of its depth.

We know that God has been preparing all the saints for these times in many ways; however, it is so unfortunate that many are called but few are chosen. The Bible tells us that there will be a great falling away from the church in the last days. Many saints have decided to give up the fight. It appears that God's way isn't good enough now after He's proven Himself repeatedly. His Word tells us that in the last days, men shall become lovers of themselves more than lovers of God. To ignore God's Word and to walk away from Him puts one in a dangerous place.

As I said from the beginning, I'm sitting here thinking, mainly because the whole world is under attack by a deadly killer virus called COVID-19. Millions are being infected, and millions are dying. My husband, Bishop Goodman, quoted, "God allowed some to be infected so that all can be affected." I said to myself, "My God, what a powerful quote!" To me, this is like God telling the saints that have been studying and hearing His Word, "I TOLD YOU THIS WAS COMING!"

Satan is desperate because he knows that he has a short time to gather more recruiters. He must come through the saints by any means necessary to get to the main target, who is ultimately, the Pastor/the Shepherd Himself. There are also other targets, ones that God has chosen to walk with the Pastor in leadership to help spread His gospel— but the Pastor is the main target. Satan doesn't want to just be in the kingdom—he wants to live in the Castle.

My previous books were called *First Lady on the Run*, but God clearly spoke to me and told me to stop being a "First Lady on the Run" and prepare for *war*! This book is not meant to be directed specifically toward you or your situation, but to just show you how the devil will use you and the ones that you hold dear to your heart as collateral damage to get to his main target, the Pastor.

Collateral damage is injury inflicted on something or someone other than the intended target. This is an unintentional damage that wasn't really aimed directly at you, but because you were in the way of the target, you were injured.

Your injury maybe critical at times, and other times, you may just get a bump on the head. If you are in the line of fire, you are bound to get hit.

Sometimes you feel like the main target because of the spiritual, emotional, physical, and mental pain that you have had to endure; but God will never leave you alone. Understand, you don't have to be related biologically to your pastor or his family; but if you are a strong believer and you really know the true power of prayer, and you are being guided by a true leader, your pastor becomes a threat to Satan, and you are subject to become collateral damage. I will also talk about how becoming a distraction to your leader can cause others to fall into collateral damage.

We must trust God through it all; however, it is also important that we trust the Shepherd that God places over us. How can we trust God and not trust His mighty acts?

At the end of 2019, my faith was really tried, and there were many times I didn't understand. But when it seemed that I was drowning and going under for the very last time, I trusted God and I still do. Now it is 2020, and God has given me 20/20 vision for my life and has revealed to me the reason for going through the pain that I had to endure.

After reading this book, hopefully you will determine if you are collateral damage or the main target.

1

Child's Play

All church folk at one time or another is guilty of participating in child's play. One of the first series that our bishop taught was titled Child's Play. I was absolutely surprised about some of the things that he mentioned in this series. Some things really blew my mind, particularly how we saints do things in church and out of church without taking a second thought.

Decisions bring things into existence. Let's take for example the statement, "I want what I want!" There's something about always wanting to have your way. The first childish act occurred in heaven when Lucifer got jealous of God and convinced a third of the angels that they didn't need God. The second childish act occurred in the Garden of Eden when Satan convinced Eve to eat the forbidden fruit, after which she was able to convince Adam to eat. Adam and Eve were both collateral damage because Satan's shots were aimed at God. I guess you ask, "What does this have to do with us and collateral damage?" Well, keep reading, and everything will come together.

The foundation of training up a child is to "Honor thy father and mother: that thy days may be long upon the land which the LORD thy God giveth thee" (Exod. 20:12 KJV). The problem with so many young people today is that they use the excuse that their parents did not raise them, or they had no one to teach them. My response is "God always has a ram in the bush."

Childhood is the stage or time of immaturity. The Bible says in 1 Corinthians 13:11, "When I was a child, I spoke as a child, I understood as a child, I thought as a child: but when I became a man, I put away childish things." When I was a child, childish things were expected of me; I also didn't see danger as grown-ups saw it. "When I *was* a child" means childishness should be a thing of the past.

Let's talk about play for a moment. To play is to handle or treat anyone lightly, to do something often out of fun or to deceive or play tricks. Another definition is to amuse. To be a child is to be fleshly. Satan enjoys playing with the saints of God. He loves getting reactions out of you. Life has many challenges, and without God in your life, it's even more challenging.

The enemy will try and toy with your emotions at your weakest points and make light of your situations as if they are not important. For example, you may be going through some emotional difficulties in your marriage. If you used to drink alcohol, he may send one of your old partners to console you and offer you a onetime drink to help numb your emotional pain. He will then sit back to see your response.

He assumes that your heart is filled with guilt. Then he proceeds to condemn you, hoping that you will continue numbing yourself again and again until eventually you will give in to him. This is not the time to have a pity party. Instead, you should do the opposite of what the enemy expects. Repent, shake the devil off, call him the liar that he is, and continue on doing the work that God has created you to do. Now, the last laugh is on the devil. All of this was a game for Satan to try and show God how easy it is to fool the saints of God.

Do you really think that Satan can fool God? I don't really think he thinks he can, but that doesn't stop him from trying because he is very persistent. The Word of God says, "The thief comes only to steal and kill and destroy" (John 10:10 NIV). You must always guard your heart from the enemy's foolish games and realize that they are just his tactics to try and get you to turn away from God.

Satan will use anyone to get you offtrack. He will try and cause conflict with the people that love you and that you have always loved. When people are spiritual, there shouldn't be any conflict that can't be resolved unless one is playing the role as a mature saint, and eventually God will pull the cover. There are so many people walking around looking like a grown-up but walking like a child. Is that someone you?

2

Let the Games Begin

So many times, people come in and out of our lives for various reasons. Only God knows why. Everything that happens in our life is no surprise to God. When trials come, we sometimes wonder and ask the question, "Why me, Lord?" Many times, I've gotten the answer, "Why not you?"

I thought I had gotten to a point where I could stop asking God questions and just begin praising Him in the midst of my trials. At the very time that I thought that things were in a good place and I felt really free to praise God, that's when Satan's games began. Satan knows when he needs to be bold, and he knows when to be passive. He knows when it's just the time to put on his sheep's clothing.

That's why the Word tells us to watch as well as pray. Beware of Satan's sneak attacks. Remember he's out to get the saints of God. He has disbursed generals, admirals, and his topnotch angels. No matter who you are, you are not exempt from Satan's subtle and strategic attacks. Always remember, he can only do what God allows.

I was ministering to the people, doing what I love doing, singing and praising God, when the enemy launched a sneak attack on me. The devil is very patient. He will devise a plan and stick to it. He will not deviate from his plan for one moment. That is unless you force him to; he depends on you to help him follow his plan through.

We have to know that God has a perfect plan for our life, even if it involves Satan's little so-called plan. That's why it's important to put all of our trust in God, even when we don't understand. God will sometimes give us a glimpse of things to come in our future to let us know that they will eventually be a part of our past.

God whispered to me, "It's time for a new testimony." So the time came for me when the game really began. I love ministry, and every opportunity that I get a chance to minister to someone, that's what I do.

My husband too is dedicated to the kingdom of God. His whole reason for living is to serve God and to be a great leader of the flock that God has entrusted him with. Not only does he love God and his people, but he also loves his family. God has empowered him with phenomenal gifts. He's been given the gifts of teaching, knowledge, and wisdom.

We know that Satan wants people to be confused when it comes to God's Word. He knows that people will die due to a lack of knowledge and understanding. We also know that Satan is the father of liars.

My husband and I are a team. He is the pastor, and I am the first lady. Not only am I the first lady, but I am also a part of the flock that God has assigned to him as his helpmeet. Of course, God has blessed me powerfully with gifts, and I am humbled; but I'm still under the covering of my pastor, who is the caretaker of my soul and the priest of my home.

Satan knows that our spiritual bond is too strong to separate, so he tried to form a weapon against me to get to him.

I took people under my wing because I just love people. I always give people the benefit of the doubt time after time after time again. I guess that's just my nature. Just because I don't respond to things that others see or that may be obvious to them does not mean that I don't see them. I always say that God is not a God of just *a* second chance because if that were so, in hell would I lift my eyes. I'm so glad that He's a God of *many* chances.

After being acquainted with one particular person for a few months, I saw a need to minister to them because God began to show me some evil spirits that needed to be addressed. I've never been one to be afraid of demonic spirits. Believe me; spirits will try you. First John 4:1–5 (NIV) says, "Beloved, believe not every spirit, but try the spirits whether they are of God: because many false prophets are gone out into the world."

I ministered to this person almost every day on the phone. Not only did I minister over the phone, but I also took every opportunity that I could in person. I would call out the spirits that I saw by name so that this person would understand demonic spirits can be living inside of you for so long—until they take over and you lose reality of who you are and Who you really belong to. Evil spirits only take residence because you allow them to.

I invested time and energy into this vessel because I believe that as long as a person can breathe, there is hope. John 10:10 says, "The thief cometh not, but for to steal, and to kill, and to destroy, I am come that they might have life, and that they might have it more abundantly."

Sometimes my benefit of the doubt can be to a fault. I find myself giving people more grace than God. I can't out-grace God. God will show us the handwriting on the wall, and we're still pleading for His blood! We also must understand that we cannot save Satan. We must remember that Ephesians 6:12 says, "For we wrestle not flesh and blood, but against principalities, against powers, against the rulers of wickedness in high places." I never fight against a person, but if that person wants to take ownership of any unclean spirits, there is nothing left for me to do.

After I continued to minister to this person, I also continued to show the love of God in every way; then I stopped receiving as many phone calls, and their attention was channeled to someone else that was very close and dear to me. Though the other person wasn't as strong or as seasoned as I was, God had really blessed this individual with powerful gifts and callings from birth.

We should never get so overconfident in our walk with God even if we feel that we have been called to save the world. One of my husband's nuggets from his book *A Piece of Me* says, "I know enough to know that I don't know enough." How well do I know that! I've been saved for almost fifty years, yet I still get Revelation through the Word.

The devil can form a weapon designed just for you; so he knows just who to send, what they should say, and what they should do. He knows how to push the right buttons to get the right response out of you. Satan never makes loud noises when he's trying to distract you, unless he knows that you like loud noises. He normally comes quietly, and then he starts to play games. He always chooses the games that you are familiar with, or sometimes he uses lies that will entice you. He will promise to make all of your dreams come true.

Once he gets you to forsake all for him, he knows that he's got you under his control; but even then, he doubts his own judgment because he knows that God has the last say in your life. All it takes is for you to change your mind and decide to come back home, like the prodigal son—and the enemy knows that this could be a game changer. We might go and flirt with Satan; but our home is with God, our Creator.

We must understand as saints of God that we are our brother's keeper. When one saint is hurt, we all should be hurt—because when we hurt, God hurts. We should always think about everything that we do before we make any decisions.

First, think about our Creator and how disappointed He must be. Then, think about our families and the people that have proven that they love us unconditionally and have prayed for us throughout the years. Satan has been playing games since the beginning of time. He started in heaven, and he is still doing the same thing down here on earth.

3

Mind Games

I think you can see now what can happen when you don't have your guard up against Satan. He has proven that he is the enemy. The enemy tends to play games with your mind. He plays games with the physical because, he knows what your flesh wants. He also plays games with your emotions because your subconscious knows more than your conscious knows, so he tries to get deep into your mind. Make no mistake: Satan can't read your mind, but he can speak to your mind.

He knows that the heart and the mind work together as one. His biggest motivation is when he can manipulate the mind into seeing a situation the way he wants you to see it, and then you act on it. The enemy wants to size you up for a takeover of your mind so that he can reduce your ability to think for yourself. He wants total control so that you will become his puppet. Every pure thought that you have, he will try and overrule to make you second-guess things.

He will become your "guardian." He wants you to become dependent on him for everything. Your spirit seems to always be grieved and you feel unhappy, but you can't seem to understand why. All of this is an indication that Satan has taken control over your mind, and he is trying to rob you of your soul. He told Eve that if she eats the fruit that she would not surely die, but that she will gain knowledge. Eve became curious and started thinking, which gave room for doubt.

The enemy hasn't changed his game plan; he's still using your mind to try and make you doubt God's Word. If you start thinking too much, that's when you tend to mess up. That's when you decide to make decisions that cause negative consequences. He will get you to trust him and confide in him, and then he will use everything that you told him against you and the people that you love.

He is always lurking around and waiting on you to make one mistake so he can condemn you. The devil is so cunning and manipulative. You always have to stay a step ahead of him. The only way that you can stay ahead of the devil is through the Word of God. That is why it is imperative that you know the Word, but not only know it—live it!

Let's go back to the powerful saint that was deceived, that I wrote about in chapter two who was blessed with many gifts. After the strong influence of such a dark spirit that was operating through the person that befriended her, this dear loved one of mine who is a powerful saint of God began to weaken, and her light became dimmer and dimmer until finally she gave in to the darkness. Because she took her eyes off of Jesus, the enemy made her believe that she would walk out of the darkness into a bright future.

Too much communication with the people that we are not that familiar with can pique our curiosity. They will sympathize with things that a true child of God will correct. This causes excuses that may have been in our subconscious to spring forth. Then we feel justified in moving forward. The Bible says in Proverbs 23:7, "For as he thinketh in his heart, so is he." Bishop Goodman also quoted, "You are not what you think you are. But what you *think*, you *are*."

Be reminded that everything that Jesus did, the devil always tried to counterfeit. Over 2000 years ago, people followed Jesus because they saw Him perform miracles, signs, and wonders. They also heard Him speak of love and peace. Satan has a following as well. He's trying to establish a greater army to fight in the war against the saints of God in these last days.

His goal is to try and make the nonbelievers think that all Christians are fake. This is his way of trying to get the nonbelievers to reject the Word of God. He has the power of the Internet through social media to help him prove his point. People that claimed that they would never leave God or ministry are on social media acting unseemly in front of the whole world, when only just a few months before, they were so in love with the Word. Satan is making a mockery of them and using them as a puppet to display his so-called power. But through all of that, Satan still cannot deny who the Creator is, and he can't deny that he himself is a part of the Creation of God—and the creation is not more powerful than the Creator.

Satan encourages the former believers to "be your true self," his new way of saying, "Forsake all and follow me." Wow! I just find it hard to believe that people can be so concerned about their dreams and so self-centered. How can you forget the Word of God that kept you for so long? How can you forget about a wonderful God that loved you in spite of all of your faults? How can you turn your back on your Creator because someone angered you?

We were created to *praise* God! If you keep that in mind, whatever desires that you have will come into fruition. The earth is the Lord's and the fullness thereof. Let everything that have breath praise ye the LORD! Psalm 37:4 says, "Delight thyself also in the LORD; and He shall give thee the desires of thine heart." This simply means to rest in the Lord and wait patiently for Him, and whatever you desire in your heart, He will give it to you. But be careful of what you desire because God is a God of order.

Whenever things are not in God's divine order, it leads to a catastrophe, and it causes a domino effect. This is another game that the enemy likes to play. The domino effect is when something is shifted or moved, and it affects other things that is in close proximity.

Satan wants to convince us to believe that whatever we decide to do with our life is our business, and we should never let anyone control us. The fact of the matter is that his ultimate goal is to manipulate and then to take total control of our mind.

If you are living on this earth, you are going to be controlled by someone or something. You cannot do anything and everything that you want to do because we all are governed by the laws of the land. Now, if you do what you want to do, there are consequences (for example, jail time)! We will be held accountable for the evil that we do. One day we will have to stand before God, and I certainly want to hear Him say, "Well done, my good and faithful servant. Well done."

4

The Danger of Playing Church

Some Christians are like a ticking time bomb. When you take your eyes off of Jesus, Satan immediately starts to speak to your mind. Instead of rebuking that fowl spirit and sticking with the truth, you began listening to his lies. As our bishop always tells us, "A lie needs a home, but the truth stands alone." The enemy always catches you when your mind is idle, and his strategy is to try and fill it with as much deceit as he can. That's why it is so important to keep your mind stayed on Jesus.

He will have a conversation with your mind to try to convince you of things, like how you are always in church and very seldom miss any services, how you always give up things that you want to do for the sake of ministry and your family, how you're a good wife and mother or good father and husband, how you are very gifted and talented, and how you do have a call on your life.

He will also question you with things like, *Why are you wasting your time to help others get ahead and doing nothing for yourself? It's time for you to shine.* He wants to convince you that if you go with him, he will help you follow your dreams. He will also promise you that once you make it big, then you can come back and retrieve the things and the family that you left behind. Sound too good to be true, right? Remember who you are having a conversation with: the father of liars. He comes as an angel of light, appearing to give advice as if he's trying to help promote your spiritual growth.

When you really love God, the very first thing that you tend to think about is how God gave His only begotten Son, how His Son gave His life for us so that we can live! Why would we not want to sacrifice dreams to be sure that God is getting all the glory and honor that's due to Him? We may have desires, but if we just trust God and put him first, He will give us the desires of our heart. Remember that after all is said and done, God is the giver of life!

I've talked about Satan and how he plays games and tries to control the mind. Now let's switch gears and talk about the saints of God. As I said previously, there will be a great falling away of the saints in the last days. This can be found in the second chapter of 2 Thessalonians.

We think *everything* evil that happens in our life is of Satan. Some of us are quick to say, "The devil made me do it," or "The devil caused this to happen!" This is *not* always so! The reason why some leave from under their solid covering to take more time for themselves and to follow their dream (that will end up being a nightmare) is simply because they listened to Satan and made a choice.

Satan puts the idea on the table and makes it look good. Some fall for it and decide to eat and digest it. The first bite tastes good, but as you keep eating, you begin to see and feel the side effects. Believe me. Everything that tastes and looks good is not always good for you.

One of the most powerful words in the Bible is *let*. It's a small word, but it has a powerful meaning. The enemy cannot do anything, control any situation, or harm you unless you *let* him. He can only do what you allow. Now, there are some things that are inevitable because it's a part of God's plan and He allows it. God will not put more on you than you can bear. When God allows Satan to come at you in a big way, just know that God's got your back and something good is coming out of it on your behalf.

God is all knowing and all-powerful. He already knows the results, but there are some that think that they are invincible and untouchable. So God has to let them know that no one is exempt from the enemy's tricks. Satan was able to convince one-third of the angels in heaven. What do you think his goal is now? That's why we need to pray without ceasing. Second Timothy 2:15 says, "Study to show thyself approved unto God, a workman that needeth not to be ashamed, rightly dividing the work of truth."

The enemy wants you to believe you can be a magician. He makes you think that you can pull the tablecloth right from under the dishes without breaking one; and you try it because it sounds so easy, but you end up breaking every dish. Those dishes are the hearts of people that love you. Whenever you are thinking about making a choice, always consider God first, and then the people that God has placed in your life.

Think about the effect that your decision will have on the people that love and depend on you. Think about that one time in your life you depended on some of the same people. Ask yourself these questions, "What would I have done if they made the same decisions and choices in life that I made? How would their choices have affected me?" Every choice that we make in life always affects someone else one way or another.

God orchestrated it this way. It is so important that we consider one another's heart. The heart is very fragile, and that's why God takes such good care of those who have dedicated their lives to serving selflessly and proving their love for Him. This is why it is said so boldly in Psalm 105:15, "Touch not mine anointed and do my prophets no harm." Warning comes before destruction!

It was hard for me to understand how the devil could possibly have such a hold over such a dear and important person in my life. Then I realized that the Word says in Matthew 24:24, "For there shall arise false Christs, and false prophets, and shall show great signs and wonders; insomuch that, if it were possible, they shall deceive the very elect."

Don't get me wrong. The saints don't just instantly believe these lies, and some saints are not so easily persuaded. This is sometimes a challenge for Satan, but remember, he is patient and he will keep trying until he realizes that he's either winning or losing.

Satan has many forms. He will come as a prophet. He will use someone that he knows has that particular gift. There are many gifts and callings that are mentioned in the

Bible. In Ephesians, prophet is one of the fivefold ministry gifts. Some have the gift without repentance. They are referred to as psychics, mediums, or fortunetellers. There are many scriptures in the Bible that mention soothsayers, which is synonymous for what we call today psychics.

When this spirit dresses up and camouflages, it looks like a Christian, acts like a Christian, seemingly knows the Word like a Christian; so most presume that they are a Christian. The big tell is when you continue to keep watching and praying. You will eventually see that they can't truly live like a Christian because the Spirit of God does not dwell in an unclean place. This is when you can recognize them to be a false prophet.

False prophets can be very impressive. What they say to you can be right on point. Some saints feel like they are hearing directly from God. Remember, they do have a gift, but it's a gift without repentance. We need to be mindful with whom we spend our time. Ask questions when you meet people. Be watchful and be aware of people that can't stay in church long.

In every church, there are people who really love God, some who like Him, and some who don't like Him. The last are the type of people called predators. If you are not watching, these people will come like a thief and rob your very soul. Some people in the church see the thief and won't do anything about it because the thief has already started working on them.

Some people of God never change their routine, perhaps thinking that the enemy won't surprise them. Satan has watched them for years. He knows everything about them. He has studied their past mistakes. He knows how and who helped them to overcome their hard times. You need to become unpredictable so that Satan won't know your every move.

If you are not sure about a person or if you haven't been around them long enough to really know them, pray and ask God for guidance, or seek advice from your shepherd when it comes down to friendships or relationships. Pray and ask God for more spiritual discernment. You don't want to have been in ministry for years, yet when the Lord returns, you find out that you've become a part of the walking dead that never regained life.

5

Self-Destruction

In this chapter, I want to talk a little about ODP, which stands for *oppression*, *depression*, and *possession*. This is a part of the enemy's strategy to control your mind. This is also the way Christians can go on Self-Destruct mode.

Oppression is when you are under mental pressure or distress. This gives you a feeling of inferiority. Satan wants you to feel that everyone thinks that you are worthless. He will continually get you alone and speak to your mind and tell you that everybody is exceeding in their gifts but not you. He tells you that everyone is getting recognition but not you. He may say, *You have way more talent and ability than most people that are in this church, and it seems as though you are being completely ignored.*

Then your idle mind starts to think. As I mentioned in the previous chapter, you know what happens when an idle mind thinks too much. You slowly begin to separate yourself from everybody that cares about you. You start believing the lies that the enemy is feeding you. Because of negative situations that are presently occurring in your life, your mental ability becomes pressured, and your mind go into a distressed mode.

This usually can happen in a marriage and between parents with teenage children. This can also happen with life's issues and even sometimes in ministry. You slowly start feeling a desire not to be around anybody but just that one person that seems to understand you. Because you have shared some of your most challenging experiences with them, they always seem to agree and say, "I understand. Been there, done that." No matter what you say, they always claim to have been through the same thing. This then gives you a sense of security and trust in this particular individual. You are convinced that no one else could possibly understand what you are feeling, no one but this person.

You may have had issues years ago that you were healed and delivered from, but Satan will try and resurface them along with guilt to make you feel even worse. Whenever you feel yourself getting oppressed in ministry, immediately talk to someone that you know is strong in the Lord. They will help you to pray through this bump in the road. Because this too will pass.

If you need to talk, be sure to talk to someone that you know that's going to give you the truth and not agree with everything that you say or feel. You must be completely honest with this man or woman of God in order to get past any obstacle. More importantly, you must be honest before God because God sees your heart, and only He can fix you if you want to be fixed.

When you have had a personal relationship with God and you know Him as your Lord and Savior, you know that there is nothing too hard for Him. Your big problem is small to Him. No matter how we feel, we must trust God on this journey and believe God for our victory! Remember, God has not given us the Spirit of fear, but of power, and of love, and of a sound mind.

The enemy is desperate to destroy the strong pastors. Destroy the pastors; destroy the sheep! He is especially targeting first families because he knows the pastors' first work begins in the home, so that's where the devil wants his main distractions to come from, the home.

Please don't go to your leader for sound advice if you're not being completely honest and open. If you want issues addressed with the truth coming straight from the Word of God, go with an open heart, and be willing to tell the whole truth and receive the truth.

Perhaps you decided not to talk to anyone about any issues, mainly because you were advised not to by your more-than-understanding friend. Before you decide to make any decisions, always remember Psalm 1:1, "Blessed is the man that walketh not in the counsel of the ungodly, nor standeth in the way of sinners, nor sitteth in the seat of the scornful." If you know God, you know where you should go when seeking Godly counsel. The Word of God has the answer to everything that you need.

Never seek counsel from anyone that's questioning their own salvation or anyone that you have been trying to minister to. If you do, it means that you really don't want the truth—you just want to hear what makes you feel good or to justify what the enemy has been feeding you.

Perhaps you've never been completely honest and openly shared your heart with anyone but this newfound friend. Perhaps when the saints that used to encourage you come around, you want to go the opposite way because you don't feel close to them like you used to; this probably even applies to your family. If this is the case, this means you are oppressed!

Depression is when you have a feeling of inadequacy and guilt, which is accompanied by a lack of energy, a lack of appetite, and lack of sleep. Most people that are depressed have a feeling of severe despondency. They isolate themselves in their homes. They go cold turkey and completely stop coming to church for no apparent reason. If they do decide to give a reason, it's usually due to some form of sickness.

The enemy definitely wants to get you to the stage of depression. This is a stage of sadness, feeling down, having a loss of interest or pleasure in daily activities. They stay away from their friends and family that they normally talk to on a daily basis. They only communicate with the one person that has made them feel comfortable, their newfound friend and soul partner; and nobody else seems to matter. Their loyalty to this person seems unshakable.

The Word clearly tells us in Exodus that God is a jealous God. Thou shall have no other gods before Him. It's terrible to fall into the hands of an angry God! When Christians experience a state of depression, this could mean that the devil has been working on them for a while.

It is so important to live in a Christian home, where the husband and wife know how to come together and fight for each other. There have been times when the enemy tried to come at me and my husband. We stood flat-footed against the devil, rebuked him, and refused to allow him to enter into our home. He has tried, but because of our individual love for God, the strength that we have together is unbreakable. There is no back door or window that he can sneak into, and he knows that.

So now he is coming at us by any means necessary. He's using my family and my health, and he's coming through anybody that he thinks that will ultimately distract me or destroy me as collateral damage. He's using me as possible collateral damage because he knows how much my husband loves me and how much I mean to him. But there's one thing he forgot: how much my husband loves God, and how much his call means to him because he's on a mandate from God. Nothing—absolutely nothing—will distract him from his assignment.

I refuse to allow Satan to make me a distraction because I'm determined to stay focused on my assignment, as well as on being my husband's helpmeet. I know that my husband, Bishop Goodman, is the target and has been for years.

Now that God has taken me to another place in Him, I'm even more of a threat to Satan. He should know by now that his tactics still won't work. You cannot let the enemy have his way in your home because he will not walk in your doors and say, "Hey, everybody, I'm your enemy!" He will quietly take up residence, make himself comfortable, and wait for chaos to hit your home like dynamite.

When you see the enemy attacking your spouse, it is no time to reason. It's time to *fight* with all your might and stomp on the enemy's head! The fight should start when you first see any signs of oppression in your home. Never invite the devil into your home, even if you know that you are strong enough to fight for the vessel that he is trying to control at that time. Do not be deceived by the enemy.

Possession is the state of having, owning, or controlling something. This is when the enemy has completely taken control of the mind, the soul, and the body. At this point, a person has completely sold out to Satan.

This doesn't necessarily mean that these people have rituals or anything like that, but a lot of their beliefs are totally different and sometimes are identified as cults because they are easily brainwashed. They have been convinced by Satan that they can live like they want and still make it into heaven. They have many definitions of what heaven is and where heaven is. Most of them dress dark and like to cover their eyes. Its's been said that the eyes are the gateway to the soul. The enemy doesn't like to look a true saint of God straight in the eyes because they can see straight through the person and see the demon for who he really is.

When a person is possessed, they believe in their theories and create their own interpretation of the Word. Satan knows the Word of God—remember, he once lived in heaven. He knows the rules. He broke them and got kicked out. Now he wants to get as many here on earth as possible to break them so we will never make it to heaven. He is upset because God got intimate with man and breathed the breath of life into him, and as a result, man became a living soul.

Satan has been out to get man from the beginning. God made man a little lower than angels, but God has given man power through the Holy Spirit to rebuke Satan and all of his tricks. We relinquish the power that God has given us when we allow Satan to deceive us with his lies, to convince us that his power is greater than the power that God has placed inside of us. The enemy is always trying to show us a better way when in reality, he doesn't have the power to show us anything. He only has the power that we give him.

When you allow Satan to control you, it can be to the point that you become *self-destructive*. You invite the enemy into your home, take his coat, let him spend the night, let him sleep in the guest room, let him bring his toothbrush...and before you know it, he's moved in. Now you have destructive relationships in your home, destructive relationships with your friends, destructive relationships in your church—and all of this was caused by you, by your decisions.

God is not the author of confusion. First Corinthians 14:33 says, "For God is not the author of confusion, but of peace, as all churches of the saints." The devil did not make you do any of this. This was all your choice. Even in a depressed state, you still can reach way down inside where the Word resides, pack your problems under your feet, and still come out undefeated. You also have brothers and sisters in the Lord that are strong enough in the Lord to pull you out of that ODP. You got a pastor and family to help you.

God has given us so many ways to escape the devil. Of course, he will sometimes knock us down, but God has given us the power the get back up again and continue the fight. So stand up and fight the good fight!

6

Weapons of Mass Destruction (WMD)

It is definitely time to fight like never before! If the devil can get the Saints of God to self-destruct just by speaking to their mind, he feels even more empowered. Satan knows that this war is not going to be easy, so he doesn't fight fair. He uses weapons of mass destruction, which I will refer to as WMD throughout the book.

WMD are weapons that can destroy entire cities, regions, etc. I consider COVID-19 a WMD because of the sheer loss of life that this virus has caused. This is a part of the Word of God through prophecy that's being fulfilled in these last days.

Satan is not using chemical, biological, or nuclear bombs to try and destroy the saints of God because he knows killing the body will not destroy the soul. He will use spiritual WMD to try and devise sneak attacks against the body of Christ. He wants to take down as many Christians as possible because he wants the body of Christ destroyed.

Peace is what God desires, but it is also written in the third chapter of Ecclesiastes, "To everything there is a season, and a time to every purpose under the heaven." The eighth verse says, "A time to love, and a time to hate; a time of war and a time of peace." If you notice the scripture says "a time *to* love and a time *to* hate." *To* means that we are in control. Then it says "a time *of* war and a time *of* peace." *Of* means they are beyond our control.

There is a spiritual warfare going on right now against the body of Christ. The saints of God must stand together and fight against Satan and his protégés. This war is inevitable, but we have the victory through Christ Jesus! According to Revelation 6:8, during the tribulation period, four horsemen will be released to conquer and kill. With war will come conflict, hostility, economic disaster, diseases, and widespread death. Romans 3:10 says, "None is righteous, No not one." The world will be filled with sin and hate. War is unavoidable during the time of tribulation.

We see the prelude in the present days of what's soon to come. I can clearly see the signs of the time, but what we are seeing now is only the beginning of sorrows. It's not over yet. Don't be deceived in thinking that the last days and the end-time are the same. Mathew 24:6 says, "And you will hear of wars and rumors of wars, see that you are not alarmed. For this must take place, but the end is not yet."

Jesus talks to his disciples about the end-time. He said that there would be rumors of wars. He is not telling them that they're the only indication of the end-time because war has been going on since the beginning of time. This is just one of the many signs that He mentioned. We are living in the last days before the end-time. No matter what wars or rumors of wars are going on around us, our mission should stay the same; and that mission is to stay focused and follow whatever Jesus says.

As we know, Jesus is a reliable predictor of the end-time. He has given us instructions and a road map to follow. So follow His instructions, and the Gospel of Jesus Christ will be proclaimed throughout the entire world—and then and only then will the end come.

Satan knows that some of the saints are going to be caught up to meet Him in the cloud during the Rapture, and he's trying to stop as many as possible before that great trumpet sound! This is why he's pulling out the biggest and most powerful weapons imaginable to try and destroy as many Christians as possible. One of his major WMD is *hate*. If he can get us to hate one another, then he knows that's half of the battle. Another one of his WMD is *jealousy*, and then the ultimate is *mind control*.

The enemy finally got full control of this woman of God that I love so dearly. Because I know the loving person that she was, I still have hope, but I have given her to God. I know that she is in good hands. I can't possibly love her more than the One that created her.

She wanted nothing else to do with her family. The enemy convinced her that everyone in her family was against her, and to her it appeared that they became her enemies. She distanced herself from them and would not visit their homes. Can you imagine how they must have felt? They were always a very close-knit family and seemed to have such close family bonds. You would think that nothing and no one could ever break them apart.

Remember, I said previously that this was a mighty saint in the army of God, but Satan has no respect of person. It is so important that we keep our minds stayed on Jesus at all times. He is waiting to snatch your mind the moment that he can distract you and get your attention. He can be a distraction in church through someone sneezing, which makes you miss something that was said in the Word that you really needed. After the sneeze, someone sitting next you may start a conversation. When you find yourself being easily distracted with something as simple as a sneeze, immediately began to pray. This may sound petty; but the enemy is desperate, and he's looking for any avenue to get into your mind.

Resist the devil, and he will flee. You have to learn to recognize the enemy when he tries to tiptoe into your mind. So much can easily distract you. The enemy seems to be grasping for straws because he never seems to put the whole puzzle together. The piece that he completely left out that's so essential is that most of the family of this individual are powerful parts of the body of Christ, and they all believe in the power of prayer!

Satan is coming against the saints in a big way. Prayer is more powerful than any weapon of mass destruction. God can ultimately control any human or spirit that tries to use any form of WMD against His people. Our prayers serve in powerful ways to change any plans that Satan has devised against us. Some people trust in words, some in threats, some in lies, and some in the enemy's promises. But I must trust in the Lord, our God. His Word says, "No weapon formed against me shall prosper." When God says it, I believe it.

7

Ready, Aim, Fire!

You know about the games that the enemy tries to play with your mind. It's time for the body of Christ to pull out your weapons that you have not used in a while and clean them up and get ready, aim, and fire. In other words, it's wartime!

Ephesians 6:11 says, "Put on the whole armour of God, that ye may be able to stand against the wiles of the devil." There is no need to put on armor if there is no war. The next verse tell us "For we wrestle not against flesh and blood, but against principalities, against powers, against the rulers of the darkness of this world, against spiritual wickedness in high places." This clearly tells you that the war that you are fighting is a war that doesn't require you to use live ammunition, guns, swords, or knives. This war requires you to use the spiritual weapons that God has given us. Put on the whole armor of God so that you may be able to withstand in the evil day—and having done all to stand, *stand*!

If you pay close attention, you can usually tell when possession has taken place in a person. They become very combative about the Word of God, and they use it for justification for what they have chosen to do. Everyone seems to have an opinion when it comes down to the interpretation of the Word. But the Word is not based on logic—the Word of God is *truth*.

For everything that the Pastor says, someone always have a *but*. Here is a good example: If the pastor says, "I want the church to fast from 7:00 AM–12:00 noon." Somebody may argue, "I heard the pastor say that he wants us to fast, *but* I can't fast that early. I take my medicine in the mornings. Pastor needs to have compassion. The Word says, 'Do unto others as you would have them do unto you'!" This person is quoting the scripture to justify his or her not wanting to fast.

God will have you do something just to show the unbelievers that you are willing to trust and obey Him. You must be *ready*! When the devil speaks to your mind and tells you that you can't fast and gives you an excuse why, tell him that Jesus is your doctor and your medicine; and you expect your healing when you finish fasting. When the enemy comes to you with excuses and doubts, speak the Word with confidence. Let the devil know who you are and Whose you are. You must first know your own value. Know who you are. You are a child of the Highest God.

You must believe what you speak. You must keep your mind stayed on Jesus. Don't let anyone give you their opinion when it comes to the Word. Keep your spiritual eyes *aimed* on Jesus! Speak the Word in and out of season. Don't be afraid to proclaim God's Word. Let it roll from your tongue like *fire!* The Word will burn any spiritual impurities away, and pure gold will shine through.

You know that the enemy is not going to stop just because you are fighting back. The reason you were told to put on the whole armor of God is because Satan is coming harder and harder; and he is recruiting more and more, preparing for the end-time. In the last chapter, I talked about WMD. I've explained what you need to do to get ready and how to aim and fire. When Satan speaks to our mind and we rebuke him with the Word of God, this is when he commands his generals to start firing. You have been given instruction on how to protect yourself from the enemy when this happens.

Ephesians 6:14–18 tell us how to prepare for the enemy's attack:

> ➤ Stand therefore, having your loins girt about with *truth*
> ➤ Having on the breastplate of *righteousness*
> ➤ Your feet shod with the preparation of the gospel of *peace*
> ➤ Above all, taking the shield of *faith*; wherewith ye shall be able to quench the fiery darts of the wicked
> ➤ The helmet of *salvation*
> ➤ The sword of the *Spirit*, which is the Word of God

Further instructions say, "Praying always with all prayer and supplication in the Spirit and watching thereunto with all perseverance and supplication for all saints."

This is our protection against the enemy. Always remember, good soldiers get wounded, but God's soldiers get good rewards.

Don't think that the devil is not sitting in a position of aim, ready, fire as well. Sometimes I think that he is in position more than the saints of God. It's almost like he has radar.

It seems like time the devil thinks that you are in a place of peace, he tries to stir up havoc. What the enemy doesn't seem to understand is that when there is chaos in the life of a true saint of God, there is still peace. But Satan will want you to always think about your issues.

When someone strays from the fold, of course you pray for their protection; you even worry at first. Even though you trust God, there is still a human side of you that has emotions and feelings. The emotional side tells you to cry, hurt, be sad. Sometimes it will tell you to lash out at God. But one thing I know about God: He can handle our anger because he knows our heart.

Satan will command his strongest demons to cast you into the fire and turn up the heat seven times hotter than normal. Your flesh will tell you to run and get out of the fire, but running only makes the fire burn faster. You must know that before Satan sent his strongest demons to get you, Jesus was already there with you. In the middle of the fire, He is still with you. As a matter of *truth*, He will never leave you nor forsake you.

Bishop Goodman preached a sermon titled "Faith Revealing Fire." The fire situations that the devil threw at you will reveal the fire that you have inside you. Haven't you heard the saying, "Fight fire with fire"?

Looking back on my loved one, I remember hearing the Word of God rolling off of her tongue like fire and seeing the manifestation of the Holy Ghost moving in her life. I've seen her receiving on behalf of her family through faith. She and I would talk on the phone as she shared prophetic dreams that God would give her. I could see the move of God right before my eyes.

I could see the direction God was taking her in. I could see the road that God was leading her to, but when the enemy's fire came, she made a detour. There was something that Satan said that mesmerized her, hypnotized her, convinced her to take her eyes off of what was the most important to her. Curiosity got the best of her.

Everything that God had blessed her with slowly dwindled away without her even realizing it. She became so caught up in selfish gain until she lost her vision, her true faith, her family, and ultimately her truth that God gave her to inspire so many others to come to Christ.

We have to be ready at all times. Thinking about my friend, I realize that it could've been me. It would've been me if it wasn't for the Lord! Be watchful and aim at Satan. Don't allow him to come with a sneak attack. Ask God for direction, and don't let your fire burn out—because if it does and you fall, you may never recover.

8

You Don't Know Me

In these last days, the body of Christ might as well get ready to go through spiritual warfare, one after another. You must go through them as saints of God and proclaim boldly and with authority, "Satan, you don't know me!" Know that Jesus is with you through every situation. Know that He will never bring you to any situation that He can't take you through and then bring you out of. What a mighty God we serve!

First things first: you must trust Him. It's easy to say that you trust God, but do you really *trust* God? There have been many times that my trust was put to the test. I'm definitely a woman of faith. Faith is one of my main manifestation gifts. I truly believe if you desire something from the Lord, you can speak, believe, and then receive from God. True believers don't just ask for selfish things; they usually want spiritual things or something in order to be a blessing to someone else.

This has always worked for me. Sometimes, when I don't want to wait on God, I would move in error. But when I ask and be patient, it will come to pass. I have been through all types of pain in my life. Some were physical, some were emotional, and some were spiritual. But this particular pain was worse than all three put together.

I didn't understand what I could have done for God to allow all of this hurt to come to me at one time. It was something I didn't want to share because I knew that it would also hurt others, so I kept it inside—and it kept tormenting me.

I asked God, "Is this some kind of test that I have to go through? Is there something that I didn't do that I should have done? Or is it something that I did that I should not have done? Had I overstepped my faith and did something arrogantly? Whatever it is God, give me the strength to go through."

God finally released me to share it with my husband, and when I was able to open my heart to him, he explained that this whole attack was not about me. He then prophetically spoke and said that God was getting ready to promote me spiritually, and this was part of the promotion process. I realized at that point that this was not just a surface promotion, but this was something that I had to feel in the core of my soul in order to be effective in what God was preparing for me to do.

Everything is ultimately directed at the leader. My husband is the pastor, and sometimes God has a shield of protection around the shepherd because He is keeping him preserved for the flock. If Satan can't get to the pastor, he will try to destroy the closest person to his heart, which in this case just happens to be me. There should be no division between the pastors and their wives because Satan wants the wives to be a distraction by causing strife in the home, which can affect the ministry.

In some churches, I've seen competition between husbands and wives in leadership to the point where it almost destroyed the ministry. Everyone has been given their own special anointing, and they're all important in the body of Christ. Remember, when it's all over, God is not going to call us by our title but by our name. "It's not what your name is. It's *where* your name is" (Bishop Goodman).

Wives, be mindful to protect your husband from situations wherein God has given you the power to handle until God releases you to share it with him. Also have a sensitive ear to the Holy Spirit. Let the Spirit be your guide.

After pouring out my soul to my husband, it seems that the devil was furious. It was almost like he started to move in fast motion. Although it felt good being released to share this pain that I was carrying, the hurt was still there in my heart. Then all of a sudden, it seemed like the pits of hell opened up, and Satan released an army of demons. It finally hit me like a ton of bricks, and every emotion that I was feeling began to surface.

After facing the reality of my loved one being snatched by Satan so subtly, I was devastated. I began to scream and cry out to God with no questions. I simply let God know that this was hard, but through it all, I was still going to trust Him.

I recognized that I was in the midst of the fire, but even then, I still trusted Him. I didn't know what tomorrow would bring, but I still trusted Him. I kept shouting,

"God, I don't understand, but I trust You! I don't know why, Lord, but I trust You!" There is nothing that Satan can do to make me not trust God.

Soon after that release, even though I was still hurting, I was at peace knowing that God was with me every step of the way. I thank God for my mother, who believes in the power of prayer. She taught me how to be a woman of faith through her example.

The saints of God were praying, and I was able to hold my head up. We may get wounded in some of the battles, but God wins all of the wars. I continued to put my trust in God each and every day. All of a sudden, things went awry with another individual that I was really praying for. I knew that they were directly affected by this woman of God that had been deceived by the devil. This dear soul began to turn on me as well. I couldn't believe it.

Is this the same person that I cried with? Is this the same person that I prayed for? Is this the same person that I talked to on the phone and encouraged night after night? Is this the same person that my husband and I constantly prayed for and cried over?

Remember when I talked about the domino effect? Well, this is a prime example of how one negative action can bring on several other negative reactions. A person can make one decision, go on about their life, and leave so many others that love them wounded forever. Just because a person does something that is wrong doesn't mean that you have to react in a negative way as it will bring reproach on your life as well. Satan convinced this wounded person to go to a place of disrespect with me, and I never would have thought I'd have to witness such darkness that lived inside this person.

Satan loves it when you have proclaimed salvation, and he exposes that dark place inside you so that he can make a spectacle out of you. His whole purpose is for you to show hate toward others, especially publicly. That really proves his theory that Christians are fake. The more I tried to show love, the more disrespect I seemed to receive. There was not just help from me alone but help from my entire family as well, but it appeared that all of the enemy's frustrations were taken out on me. The enemy never faces who he's really afraid of; he always talks to others about who intimidates him the most.

Everyone that had a problem with my husband were seemingly trying to come against me. Again, I was getting puzzled. This time I was getting angry instead of hurting. I felt myself beginning to travel to a place in my mind where I had not visited in years.

I began to time travel back into the Cookie days. Those were the days of my youth when I didn't mind expressing exactly what was on my mind; it was also when I would physically fight my way out of a lot of my problems. As I began to head back from my time travel, I realized that I'm better than Cookie. I Also realized that all these years that I've known these people that have hurt me, I need to tell them individually, "YOU DON'T KNOW ME!"

My four-year-old grandbaby used to sing, "I'm not scared because Jesus is alive." I belong to God, and His Word says in Psalm 105:15, "Touch not mine anointed and do my prophets no harm." I used to be Cookie, but she does not live here anymore. God has changed my name. You've got the right address, devil, but a new person lives here! This made me wonder if this spirit was living in this vessel the whole time.

When you see any indication that the enemy is trying to snatch someone precious to you away from you, that is when the fight begins. You never give in to the devil and turn against the ones that are praying with you and for you.

I had to accept my spiritual promotion and realize that God had all of this planned from the beginning. He had to let Satan know that I belong to Him. So if Satan wants to try and get to Bishop, He is beating on the wrong door. First Corinthians 15:58 says, "Therefore my beloved brethren, be ye steadfast, unmovable, always abounding in the work of the Lord, forasmuch as ye know that your labour is not in vain in the Lord."

9

Who Are You?

I came to realize that one of the biggest problems with some of the saints is that they have an identity crisis. They do not really know who they are in Christ, and they do not understand the power that they possess. The enemy can persuade some people to do whatever he wants them to do with not much effort on his part. The enemy can tell them that the sky is falling, and they will start running for cover without looking. That is just how vulnerable some of the saints are to whatever they hear.

Christians usually think that they are stronger than what they really are until they are put to the test. We all have different rules we play by depending on our circumstances. You could be one person at work, another person at home, another person around your friends, and a completely different person at church. How do you develop this all-important *you* to change the world?

This is what happened to my loved ones that have fallen away from the faith. It could happen to some of your loved ones and maybe even you. The problem was they got in their own way. *You* could get in your own way. So I feel that is very necessary that I talk to you about your favorite topic: you.

I want to revisit the scripture 2 Corinthians 5:17:

> Therefore if any man be in Christ, He is a
> new creature; old things have passed away,
> behold, all things are become new.

People in general are self-preoccupied beings. In most cases, church folks think everyone is focused on their situation when in reality 98 percent of the time, most people are focused on their own problems, not on the mistakes that you make (unless it affects them).

Asking yourself who you are is not as easy as you think it is. I found out during my studies that there are several *yous*:

➤ There is the *you* that people think you are.
➤ There is the *you* that you think you are.
➤ There is the *you* that you are expected to be.
➤ There is the *you* with your insecurities, desires, talents, and personality traits. This is the *you* that you live with every day that few people see.
➤ There is one more *you* that completes the picture. A *you* designed by God that is meant to outshine all of the others.

We are triune beings: each of us have a body, soul and spirit. In my studies, I found a quote that said, "We are a

Spirit, we have a Soul, and we live in a Body." This is the way we were designed by our Almighty God. Your *soul* is made up of your personality, your drive, your motivation, and your emotions.

You say that you love God, but you have lost your motivation to serve Him. What used to be exciting and uplifting to you is not working for you anymore. You do not find it hard in doing some of the things that you would not think of doing in the past. You find yourself doing what makes you feel good emotionally. You do not pray for guidance anymore because you are operating on your emotions only. You barely participate in church functions because you feel you need a break from the church people, and it seems that service is getting longer and longer each Sunday.

If you notice a personality change within you, then it's time to ask yourself the big question, "Who am I?" and really mean it because your soul is crying out. The only one that knows you better than yourself is God. Pray and ask God to restore your mind and renew your spirit.

Your *spirit* is dead before you enter a relationship with God. Ephesians 2:2 tells us that before you invite Christ into your life and heart, this spirit is inactive. When you invite Jesus into your life as your Lord and Savior, this spirit part of you is awakened! You then become a new person. The old has gone, and the new life has begun. You are still you—your memories don't disappear, and your personality doesn't disappear—but your life changes. There's a new sheriff in town, and His name is Jesus!

This new compartment in you is where you and God hang out; and this new part is hungry, not for physical food but spiritual food. It's hungry for worship, it's hungry for praise, it's hungry for prayer, it's hungry for time alone with God, and it's hungry for fellowship with the saints.

When you start to feel empty on the inside and the still small voice that used to speak to you seems to have shut down and you hear nothing, it is self-inventory time. This means that you have been starving the spirit for a long time because of strongholds! Your focus is on pleasing yourself, on following your own dreams and desires. According to Paul, this is living to satisfy your own flesh. This is when the saints put aside the feeding of the spirit man and feed their physical or emotional appetite instead. You can put yourself in harm's way and cause someone else that is really trying to protect the shepherd to suffer as collateral damage.

You can also become a distraction to many, who can end up as damaged goods because you have given up the fight. Romans 12:2 reminds us, "Be not conformed to this world: but be ye transformed by the renewing of your mind, that ye may prove what is that good and acceptable, and perfect, will of God." (This verse reminds me of the powerful person that I have mentioned throughout this book. This was her favorite scripture.)

It is so important to hear God's Word as it comes out of your mouth. The same Word that you used to draw many to Christ is the same Word that will sustain you at your most critical times. If you are so in love with the Word, it will show through in what you do. Love is *action*. It was action when God gave his Son. It was action when His Son gave His life. Philippians 4 also teaches us to order our way of thinking after God's way of thinking.

I have witnessed people that were totally dedicated to the ministry. I can honestly say that just by looking at their works and the time and effort that they put into everything that they did, I thought that they really loved God. At that time, I'm sure that they did. But if Satan can get you to listen to him and if he can get into your mind, he can make you forget who you are; and before you know it, you will become a stranger to all of the saints of God that knew you. You will no longer look the same spiritually and in some cases, physically.

By then, your mind has been changed and rearranged, and you are no longer who you used to be in Christ. So if you find yourself in this condition and you want to know who you really are, God has the answer.

I was looking at a movie, and it really inspired me to the point that I want to share this with you. If you ever have doubts about who you are, read the first chapter of Ephesians, and you will know who you really are—if you only accept it!

Who You Are According to Ephesians 1

- ✓ You are blessed
- ✓ You are chosen
- ✓ You are holy
- ✓ You are blameless
- ✓ You are loved
- ✓ You are His sonship
- ✓ You are redeemed

- ✓ You are forgiven
- ✓ You have purpose

Once you know who you are and accept who you are, you just have to *trust* God, and you *will* grow into who you are!

You must begin to take responsibility for what you allow into your mind and heart by the things you watch, read, engage in, and by the people you surround yourself with. God wants you running *to* Him whenever you can and not away from Him.

Anything and everything that you need is in Him:

- ✓ In Him is your *identity*
- ✓ In Him is your *victory*
- ✓ In Him is your *right standing*
- ✓ In Him you have your *supply*
- ✓ In Him you have your *healing*
- ✓ In Him you have your *comfort*

This is the *you* God made you to be. You are not destined to live in defeat, discouragement, debt, or defiance. Your part is knowing who God made you to be.

Romans 8:37 says, "Nay, in all these things we are more than conquerors through Him that loved us." This verse does not apply to you until or unless you claim it as your own. Speak it from your lips, and start to apply it to your daily life. Then you will begin to know who you are.

10

When You Know, You Grow!

As I look back at all of the pain—the mental, spiritual, and emotional hurt—that I've experienced throughout the years, I can truly say that they were all growing pains. As you mature in the Lord, this does not mean that you will never experience pain again, but you will be more prepared for what you must do. You will be able to go through and make it to the other side of the pain. And on the other side of pain is *joy* and *peace*.

As you are going through it, sometimes it will seem like the pain is getting stronger and harder to bear. This is very likely because bigger and stronger demons are being released to attack you. The devil will not send low-level demons to attack a mature saint. The more mature you are in the Lord, the more mature the demons are. God's people are "built God-tough."

My husband has been specially blessed by God with the gifts of knowledge and wisdom, as I previously mentioned. The gift of knowledge is knowing and understanding the Word of God in a way only God can give it to you.

The gift of wisdom is knowing what to do with the knowledge that God has given you.

Sometimes we can misuse the knowledge that God has given us. That's why it is so important to know God's Word. Second Timothy 2:15 says, "Study to show thyself approved unto God, a workman that needeth not to be ashamed, rightly dividing the word of truth. But shun profane and vain babblings: for they will increase unto more ungodliness." Not only knowing the Word is important, but showing the Word in your life is even more important. When you know, you grow! This is only possible through studying the Word of God, accepting it, and then applying it to your everyday life.

Aside from the importance of studying God's Word, there is another thing worth noting. You may recall I quoted this nugget from the book *A Piece of Me*: "I know enough to know that I don't know enough." You cannot think that you have reached a peak in studying. There is *always* fresh revelation that God constantly feeds us.

There are certain things God reveals to pastors that they cannot reveal to us immediately. When the flock is ready to digest what has been given to the shepherd, then comes the fresh revelation. The sheep never outgrow the shepherd, but some sheep are disobedient and stubborn and refuse to follow the shepherd. Why would you want to fall into a ditch when you have someone that can guide you away from the ditch and keep you from falling in?

You show growth when you can admit that you are afraid to go alone and that you need help. You show growth when you admit your flaws, when you are not afraid to be vulnerable for the sake of truth. You show growth when you stand on the Word of God even when it is not popular. You show growth when you can speak out of your mouth and rebuke Satan openly.

There are many ways to personally know when you're growing. Hebrews 6:1 says, "Therefore leaving the principles of the Doctrines of Christ, let us go on unto perfections; not laying again the foundation of repentance from dead works, and of faith toward God." In other words, you have to move beyond the elementary teachings about Christ and be taken forward to maturity.

Some people have seen themselves grow and know what it feels like to grow, yet they have given in to the wiles of the enemy. You may have loved ones in your life (as I do) or people you have really been praying for that have fallen from grace because of the choices they made. You may be the one that Satan deceived at the very time when you thought that you were far above being deceived.

Jeremiah 12:2 says, "Thou hast planted them, yea, they have taken root: they grow, yea, they bring forth: thou art near in their mouth. And far from their reins." I say to the shepherds: don't be discouraged in these last days, and don't get weary in well doing. Even though you have taught them and they stayed rooted in the church only for a season. They may have grown and brought in others. They may have always talked about how much they loved their church and pastor and that they will never leave. But then all of it was just words because it was far from their hearts. Their actions ended up saying something totally different.

The body of Christ must have a deep desire for the Word of God. It says in 1 Peter 2:2–3, "As newborn babes, desire the sincere milk of the word, that ye may grow thereby: If so be ye have tasted that the Lord is gracious." Once you have tasted the Word, you will know that the Lord is good.

Many people will try and convince you that they love the Word, but the evidence is in the way they live. You cannot change the Word to fit the way you want to live your life. You must change your life to live according to what the Word says. There is no room for compromise.

When Jesus hung, bled, and died on the cross for our sins, He did not compromise. He just did it because He knew that we needed redemption for our sins. He loves us that much.

As we know, God is Love and Truth. If He lives inside of us, that means Love and Truth reside inside of us. If you decided to turn from what you know to be the truth—not because you were told to do so but because you came across an untruth and accepted it—then at this point, you chose to believe a lie. Truth and lies cannot reside in the same place.

The Word says that Satan is the father of liars and Jesus is Love and Truth, so when your house gets dirty, Jesus will gracefully leave because He will not live in an unclean place. There is no way that you can love God and hate His people out of the same heart and think that you are a part of the body of Christ. You may be a part of *a* body, but it doesn't belong to Christ.

Just recently, I experienced a situation that caused me to really think hard about how to react. At first, my flesh thought about reacting negatively because usually our flesh is the first to react, but the Holy Spirit reminded me that I must keep my flesh under control. Then the Holy Spirit reminded me of who I am and who I belong to. I began to tell Satan out loud, "That's right, Satan. I belong to God, and I will not lower my standards by responding to my flesh. God got this!" Had I not listened to the Holy Spirit, I'm sure I would have regretted the outcome. That could have been an opportunity for Satan to use my mind, but God handled it!

Again, I say that's why it's so important that we keep our minds stayed on Jesus. Psalm 119:11 says, "Thy word have I hid in mine heart, that I might not sin against thee." His Word must take residence in your heart. The key to growth is you must *know* God and *accept* his Word.

A lot of people are just acquainted with God and have been for years, but they have never known Him as their personal Lord and Savior. In order to know Him in a personal way, you have to have a relationship with Him, which requires spending time with Him. Going to church, sitting and listening to the pastor preach on Sunday morning, maybe going to Sunday school every now and then, and going to Bible study do not serve as time spent. Some people act like going to church is a prison sentence as they constantly look at their watch to see what time it is. They worry that they will be late to do…nothing! All of this does not count as quality time with God.

There needs to be *personal* time—prayer closet time, consecration time—wherein it is just you and God. There needs to be time wherein you're not just speaking to Him but letting Him speak to your heart as well. When you don't take this time, this is when you tend to make bad decisions. You neglect to consult God about things because you think you know what His answer will be.

If you are not sure how to establish a strong relationship with God, you can start with Psalm 25:4, "Shew me thou ways, O LORD, teach me thy paths." Ask God to open your spiritual eyes so that you can see how to walk in the path that has been laid down for you.

Psalm 86:11 says, "Teach me thy way, O LORD, I will walk in thy truth, unite my heart to fear thy name." Ask God to open up your spiritual ears so that you can hear Him speaking and understand Him clearly.

Even though God knows what you are thinking, He wants you to communicate with Him verbally. He wants to hear your voice. He inhabits in the praises of His people. This is also to let the devil know you are walking in truth and that you love, honor, and fear (respect) our Lord God Almighty!

11

Better Is Forward

If you are a part of the body of Christ, I'm sure by now you have experienced going through trials and tribulations. But I can assure you that if you can hold out and trust God, better is forward. There are better things ahead for your life. The Word tells us in Philippians 3:14, "I press toward the mark for the prize of the high calling of God in Christ Jesus." As you go through life, you will always have to face obstacles, but it's good to know that better days lie ahead.

You may feel like damaged goods due to collateral damage, but God can heal you and put you back out on the battlefield. Your scars will be your testimony to others. If He did it for you, He will do it for them, if they only trust and believe.

Some people prefer to focus on their scars and hold onto their troubles. You may have been taught, that when you get to the end of your rope, to just hold on. Well, I was taught that when you get to the end of your rope, let go and God will be your safety net. He won't let you fall without catching you.

After being tried so many times by Satan, you should be able to recognize him really easily. He should not be able to make a sneak attack on you. You should be able to slam the door in his face. Better yet, don't even open the door. You need to be sure to take a self-examination so that you will know that you are in the right place in God. I can assure you that as you move forward, Satan will not give up; but always remember, "The joy of the Lord is your strength."

Our bishop teaches us that all you need is a memory. Philippians 4:8 says, "Finally, brethren, whatsoever things are true, whatsoever things are honest, whatsoever things are just, whatsoever things are pure, whatsoever things are lovely, whatsoever things are of good report; if there be any praise, think on these things."

Think about the many times that you were in trouble and God brought you out. Remember the times when you didn't have sufficient food on your table to feed your family, and He supplied you with the food. Remember when you needed a certain amount of money to pay your bills, and He gave you just the amount that you needed. Because of your faith and trust in God, you know Him to be a provider. The fact maybe that you don't have money in your pocket doesn't faze you because the truth is "my God shall supply your need according to his riches in glory by Christ Jesus" (Phil. 4:19).

Truth is the reality that lies beneath an appearance. You don't have to look like what you are going through. Stop being so predictable to the enemy. Don't follow the same routine in life. It's time to make a drastic change so that we confuse the devil. You have to strategically plan for war.

One of the greatest weapons that you have against the enemy is faith. Above all, carry the shield of faith so that you can extinguish the flaming arrows of the enemy with confidence. Hebrews 11:1 says, "Faith is the substance of things hoped for, the evidence of things not seen." Basically, faith is "when you can show before you know, you know it's going to show." This is another nugget from the book *A Piece of Me*. You have to trust that if you love God and you are one of the called, everything that happens in your life He is working out for your good.

Anything that the enemy throws at the true saints of God, he has to first get permission from God. You should be humbled and grateful with just the thought of our Creator, the Almighty God, trusting you enough to allow Satan to try you. That simply means that you must be pretty special to God. God has confidence in His children.

Psalm 30:5 says, "Weeping may endure for a night, but joy cometh in the morning." Make no mistake. You may be going through your reaping time for some bad seeds that you've sown, or you may be suffering because of disobedience. You may have self-inflicting suffering due to certain choices and decisions, which I have already covered previously.

The called are the ones that are trustworthy to God. These are the saints that have a close and personal relationship with God. When you have a pastor that is focused, you no longer have to remain in your past, and you don't need to be afraid to follow his lead as he follows God's lead.

Focus instead on being teachable. Use the knowledge that your leader is passing on to you. Ask God to give you wisdom in using the knowledge.

Some of the benefits of wisdom are:

❖ Good Judgment: Those who have wisdom can better handle the challenges that rise from leading.
❖ Strong Character: Wisdom can develop your character and positively impact others, which is needed for the everyday challenges of life.
❖ Grow Influence—Wisdom can increase your ability to influence others.

We must know who God is. He is Jehovah, the Great I AM. He created the heavens, the earth, the seas, and everything in them in six days. When He came as a man over two thousand years ago, He was named Jesus. He is coming soon with His mighty angels in flaming fire to destroy His enemies and the world.

Some people don't fear God. It shows in their actions. Fearing God is loving His commands and hating evil. Fearing God is recognizing Him as the first cause and the last end of all things. Saints of God, you must know that God is in control. He has the final say. As believers, we must have faith, belief, and trust in God.

In the fear of the Lord, God opens our eyes, ears, and heart to truth and wisdom. God opens our eyes to His Word. He shows us His secrets. We have no reason to fear no man. Wisdom cannot be found anywhere in this universe but in the fear of the Lord. So don't be afraid of the future; don't be a prisoner of your past. God knows your past, present, and future.

Whatever God has prepared for you, Satan can't stop it no matter how hard he tries. God gives us sight, even in the darkness so that we can find our way. It's like daylight in the darkness for His people. So, saints of God, I encourage you to praise God and know that you are fearfully and wonderfully made! Just trust God, and know that better is forward.

12

The Ultimate Collateral Damage

It is said in Genesis 1:1, "In the beginning God created the heaven and the earth." Every great artist signs their masterpiece. God created the heaven and the earth in five days, and on the sixth day, He created man. After creating all of the beauty that hangs in the sky, all of the colorful landscaping, the water, and animals, He then looks onto this big beautiful canvas that He had just created and saw that something was missing. He then signed His masterpiece with man as His signature. After all was done, He rested on the seventh day. Do you realize how blessed we are to be created in the image of God?

This was the beginning as we know it from Genesis, the first book of the Bible. This is when the heaven and the earth was created. There was a heaven before then. This heaven is where Satan decided to try and go against God. He convinced one-third of the angels to side with him to start a war.

I told you that Satan is consistent because he is still doing the same thing today. He tries to convince you to join forces with him because he wants to start a war against God, and he wants your soul. This makes him feel more empowered, and he knows he can't fight alone.

This situation with Satan did not move God. He sent Michael, His archangel, to handle it. Satan and the one-third that went against God were kicked out of heaven. I would have thought that being around God and knowing that He was the Creator of all of the angels should have given Satan a clue that God could have blinked an eye and destroyed him!

Before man was created, Satan was already here on earth. So Satan didn't just pop up out of thin air. He's been lurking around for a long time, waiting for an opportunity to get back at God for being thrown out of heaven. Satan wants revenge! Now that we have established who Satan is ultimately angry with, we can move on to the end of the book and on to the Ultimate Collateral Damage.

God is showing us right now in every possible way that He is about to return. He is picking out the people who want to hear the Word of God. Not everyone is going to see things the way that the Pastor sees things; but any leader expects a return on their investment, so to speak.

Think about when Jesus healed the ten lepers, and He told them to tell everyone of their healing. They were all being obedient by running out to tell others of their healing. Out of the ten, only one went back to Jesus to show gratitude and appreciation for his healing. Psalm 103:2 says, "Bless the Lord O my soul, and forget not all His benefits." God will tell you to go, but it's up to you to decide to give thanks. Sometimes you can miss out on your blessing because you never show gratitude or appreciation.

Second Corinthian 4:5 says, "All this is for your benefit, so that the grace that is reaching more and more people may cause thanksgiving to overflow to the glory of God." Even Jesus wants to know that you appreciate Him blessing you. So be thankful in all things. Never take your blessings for granted.

Being grateful will certainly benefit you, and this is a way to bless God. Be grateful for who God has placed as the caretaker over your soul. You can get a word from anybody, but you need to be pastored. God needs a navigator because He knows how to maneuver. Let your pastor know that he's investing the Word of God into a potential great leader, one that will show appreciation and continue to spread the Gospel of Jesus Christ.

Remember this: "Before you thank the priest, you must thank the King!" This is another quote by Bishop Goodman. It means you can thank your pastor publicly, but if you never thank God privately, where is your heart? I want you to understand how important it is to be grateful and appreciative for all that God has done for you from the very beginning until wherever your now is.

From the beginning, throughout the corridors of time, Satan has been patiently waiting for an opportunity to try and get back at God for having him replaced. Then came the birth of our Lord and Savior Jesus Christ. There was so much sin and corruption on earth until God had to come down to earth in the form of His Son, to be a blood sacrifice so that man can have a way of redemption. First Peter 1:18–20 says,

> Forasmuch as we know that ye were not redeemed with corruptible things, But with the precious blood of Christ, as of a lamb without blemish and without spot: Who verily was foreordained before the foundation of the world; but was manifest in these last times for you.

God gave His only begotten Son, and His Son gave His life for you and me. All of this was for us to have a way back to the Father through the blood of Jesus. This is why God inhabits in the praises of His people, and this is why the saints of God should forever be grateful and show appreciation for His loving-kindness and His tender mercies.

Satan did not want Jesus to die for our sins. This really angered him. Jesus dying on the cross gave us a choice. We were predestined to be here. You must trust God in everything. Hold on to the truth, and don't let it go. No matter how good a lie may sound, keep trusting God!

The true saints of God have been sealed with His Word, and in His own due season, He will unseal us to be with Him. Ephesians 1:13 says, "In whom you also trusted, after that you heard the Word of truth, the gospel of your salvation: In whom also after that you believed, you were sealed with that Holy Spirit of promise." Satan is trying to go inside of every church to steal as many saints as he possibly can before God unseals us to be with Him. This is also why you have to continually pray for someone other than yourself. A large part of where a person's strength comes from is in prayer.

Stay in tune with the Holy Spirit because that's how we will know what God wants us to do. It is very important that we listen closely to the Holy Spirit in these last days because Satan will present some great things before you and great opportunities. Hold on to your memory; and remember that whatever you find on this earth that is great, God is greater!

Ephesians 1:18–19 says,

> The eyes of your understanding being enlightened; that you may know what is the hope of His calling, and what the riches of the glory of His inheritance in the saints. And what is the exceeding greatness of His power to us-ward who believe, according to the working of His mighty power.

In essence, Paul is telling the saints of God that there is nothing going on, on the outside of us that can compare to what's going on, on the inside of us. Our bishop preached on this during one of the Sundays after the coronavirus outbreak, and it really blessed my soul. What a mighty God we serve!

I'm convinced that the Holy Spirit took over as Bishop Goodman was preaching. It's what I call a sermon for the last days, and He titled it "The Exceeding Greatness of His Power." He said, "God is so powerful! He sat in glory and raised Himself from the dead then placed Himself next to Himself. Now *Himself* is sitting high and looking low." How can we doubt such a powerful God?

He also said, "God is particular about His company and who sits next to Him. Are you particular about the company that you keep? Are you saving a seat for Satan every Sunday at church?"

I said all of that to let you know who Satan is really angry with. He is angry with God. First of all, it's because he couldn't be in control in heaven. Then he and his followers got kicked out of heaven. He was also jealous because God was intimate with man when he made him. Man was made from the dust of the earth, God breathed the breath of life into man, and man became a living soul.

Satan also has to ask permission to touch anyone here on earth, so he still has no control. Satan knows that he can't destroy God, so the next best thing is to try to destroy His creation. So the Ultimate "Collateral Damage" was the Son of God. Jesus served Himself as "collateral damage" in place of man, because He *decided* to, it was not Satan's choice. Let me be clear: Jesus served Himself as "collateral damage." This way, no man has to suffer like our Lord and Savior Jesus Christ had.

This was an attack directed at God. The only way that Satan thinks that he can get to God is to destroy every opportunity of man ever having a chance at redemption. I couldn't imagine going through any of what Jesus had to go through for our sins.

After Satan saw the whole process of Jesus's death and resurrection, it angered him even more. Satan knew that this would make it easier for mankind to repent for their sins. Please understand. I know that Satan cannot kill God or destroy Him; but what he wants to do is to intimidate, manipulate, and try and destroy God's creation spiritually.

Satan's goal now is to target the shepherds under whom God has assigned certain flocks in the body of Christ. The original plan was to tempt Jesus at His weakest point, which was when He was fasting in the wilderness for forty days and forty nights. Jesus's spirit would not allow His flesh to give in. Satan tried everything that He could throughout the entire process of Jesus being born until His death and resurrection.

All this only proves that whatever God orchestrates, nothing can stop. Jesus is the living Word. Now that the Son is sitting next to Him in glory and the days are numbered before Jesus's return, Satan is desperate. Satan is throwing hand grenades in every church. It doesn't matter to him who gets hurt. He is trying to be a straight shooter and hit the pastor, but if not, he hopes that the pastor is so devastated or so afraid that he will close his doors out of fear.

Among the ammunition that the devil is using are pandemics, economic collapse, poverty, unjust governmental policies, prejudices, hate crimes, wars, and everything else that he can do to stop the churches from functioning. It is time for the body of Christ to stop playing games with the enemy because the enemy is not playing games with us.

There are people that really want to be saved and want to know more about what true salvation is. There are also some that have sold their souls to Satan. Mathew 6:6 says, "Give not that which is holy unto dogs, neither cast ye your pearls before swine, lest they trample them under their feet and turn again and rend you." The enemy wants us to continue to focus on one or two people that don't want Jesus in their life instead of focusing on the ones that do.

Because of Satan's misjudgment, we have become his ultimate collateral damage. Satan will try and *distract* us anyway that he can because he can't truly destroy what doesn't belong to him. He is the father of all liars, and God has prepared a place for him and his followers. So be not deceived.

It's decision time—you must decide whom you are going to serve. Mathew 6:24 says, "No man can serve two Masters; for either he will hate the one and love the other; or else he will hold to the one and despise the other. You cannot serve God and mammon."

We live in a world of uncertainties, but we serve a God of certainty. We need to be sure to get in place and stay in place. Don't be afraid of becoming collateral damage for your pastor or shepherd. Don't be afraid to get wounded for the sake of ministry because while circumstances may change your condition, your position doesn't have to.

I would like to leave this with you, from the mouth of my bishop/husband, "We are all in this together, but are we together in all of this?"

13

Warriors, Stand Strong!

After reading the last chapter, I know that you must be visualizing in your mind the pain and suffering that our Lord and Savior Jesus Christ went through for our sins. He suffered through all of this because He *chose* to be "collateral damage" on our behalf. Whenever you think of doing wrong, think about what our Lord and Savior went through because He loved us so much. He thought about us at the cross. I myself take that personally.

When you feel weary in well doing, allow the thought of Him dying on the cross to give you strength and to recognize that you are a warrior—and that you must stand strong! If Jesus the Christ chose to be "collateral damage" for us, then you should have no problem being collateral damage for whomever He has chosen to watch over your soul. I can only imagine loving the world so much that you are willing to give up your life so that they can live.

All of the pain that you may go through now can't compare to what He went through to show His love for us. Your thoughts of doing wrong should turn into songs of praise. I want to take this time to just encourage the entire body of Christ. Thank you for being resilient and continuing the fight. Know that we are all in this together.

If you are a part of the body of Christ, I encourage you to *stand strong* on the battle line. Keep your eyes straight ahead. You are prepared, and you are equipped through the Word of God. Keep your weapons and your spirit ready at all times, and let the Holy Spirit lead you. Don't let your carnal mind start directing you because you will find yourself dancing with the devil, and he will try and take the lead every single time.

I know that sometimes it seems that God is not there. I experienced that very same feeling when Satan snatched my loved one away so quickly. I prayed and I cried out to God on her behalf. No matter how much I prayed and cried, it seemed that God wasn't answering me. I couldn't hear His voice speaking to me. I couldn't feel His presence in the room.

I went driving alone to see if He would show me a sign—maybe in the clouds, through someone's sudden movement, through a bird, or anything that would ease my mind. But there was nothing. I'm sure that you've heard it said many times, "Elvis has left the building." Well, I felt like Jesus had left the building. But I still never stopped trusting Him, and I never got angry at Him.

About two days later, we had service at our church, and I had to preside. I mentioned that I would love to have a glimpse of heaven just to feel God's presence. Nobody but God knew what this was all about. Our praise dance leader had choreographed a routine, and before they danced, she explained what it was about. When I saw this dance, God immediately began to minister to me. It was like no one else was there—just me and God.

He entered and allowed me to see the third heaven. He instructed the angels to prepare for war against Satan. God heard my cry. He was literally showing me how sometimes we pray and think that He doesn't hear us, but in truth, He's working it out. He was there all the time, getting the angels prepared to stand on the battle line against Satan, on my behalf.

When you feel like you can't hear God, know that he is there working it out on your behalf. When I saw all of this being revealed right before my eyes at the moment when I needed it most, I cried out, "Thank You, Lord!" with all of my heart and soul.

While I was looking and searching for a word from God, He was there all the time. When Jesus spoke to the disciples before He left, He said in Matthew 28:19–20,

> "Go ye therefore, and teach all nations, baptizing them in the name of the Father, and the Son, and of the Holy Ghost. Teaching them to observe all things what-soever I have commanded you and, lo, I am with you alway, even until the end of the world. Amen."

The word *lo* simply means look or see, observe, pay attention. Jesus also said that He will be "with you alway." This means that He will be with you when you know it and when you don't know it. He'll be with you when things are good in your life and when things are not so good.

Just because a person is standing by you or sitting next to you doesn't mean that they are with you. This has nothing to do with how close a person is around you or beside you. A person maybe praying for you at the moment, but that doesn't mean that they are with you.

Alway is not a typographical error in the Bible. *Alway* is specifying the spiritual distance between you and God. It doesn't matter where you go—as long as you are in God's way, He will be there. When we fall down, He picks us up; when we are weak, He makes us strong. He said He will do this even unto the end of the world.

God doesn't expect us to do everything right. He just wants us to give it our best. Don't be afraid during adversity. Be a strong soldier. God will hold you in His arms because even though you are a soldier, you are still His child.

The world will continue to charge in on you. The enemy has no sympathy for the saints of God, and likewise, we should have no sympathy for the enemy. Remember, we are empowered by the Word of God. You are not alone because God's army is standing with you, and God is standing right by your side. And He will give you peace.

The body of Christ is mighty. We must make it our priority to see Jesus by any means necessary. One day soon, Jesus is coming to take us up where we belong. He gives us strength when we are weak. He is the Gift that keeps on Giving.

Warriors, stand strong, and know that we are collateral damage. But also know that God's got us! When it's all said and done, keep in mind what's said in 2 Timothy 4:7–8:

> I have fought a good fight, I have finished my course, I have kept the faith: Henceforth there is laid up for me a crown of righteousness, which the Lord, the righteous judge, shall give me at that day and not me only, but unto all them also that love his appearing.

Continue to stay in the battle until the end. If you have battle scars, always remember that it doesn't matter how long you've been fighting or how many scars you may have. God's got you! It does not matter how long but how *strong*!

About the Author

Dr. Vera Goodman is a native of Jacksonville, Florida. After graduating from Ribault Senior High, she continued her education in Florida Community College of Jacksonville and finished with an associate's degree in computer science. Dr. Goodman also received a bachelor's degree in Christian education, a master's degree in Christian psychology, and an honorary doctorate degree in Sacred Letters, received from Jacksonville Theological Seminary.

In addition to being educated, she is the devoted and loving wife of Bishop Dr. Jan D. Goodman Sr., pastor and founder of One Accord Ministries International Inc. located in Jacksonville, Florida. Dr. Goodman is very active in the ministry and walks in her prophetic calling as Senior Evangelist and Spiritual Advisor for JDG Ministries Inc. Focusing on preaching and teaching the true Word of God, she relies on the calling God gave her at birth.

In addition to her passion for the Word of God, Dr. Vera Goodman is blessed with the gift of song. She has directed and ministered with many artists worldwide. She has produced more than five projects with award-winning choir, Bishop Dr. Jan D. Goodman Sr. and the Voices of

One Accord, and award-winning Gospel group, Anointed Praise Arukah. Dr. Goodman walks in God's purpose as a singer, producer, and arranger of Christ Lifting Music.

From her first two books, *First Lady on the Run* and *First Lady on the Run: The Journey*, Dr. Goodman shows that she is a woman of God staying on the path of multi-faceted ministry paved by God Himself.

CPSIA information can be obtained
at www.ICGtesting.com
Printed in the USA
BVHW081925230321
603272BV00008B/1080

9 781098 069391